GW00994365

NEW
MOVEMENT

How to Respond

Updated Edition

Philip H. Lochhaas

A CHRISTIAN WITNESS

CONCORDIA   PUBLISHING   HOUSE   •   SAINT   LOUIS

This edition published 2010 Concordia Publishing House.
Text copyright © 1998, 1995 Concordia Publishing House.
3558 S. Jefferson Avenue, St. Louis, MO 63118–3968

1-800-325-3040 • www.cph.org

Originally published as *How to Respond to the New Age Movement* in The Response Series © 1988 Concordia Publishing House.

Manufactured in the United States of America

Library of Congress Cataloging-in-Publication Data

Lochhaas, Philip H., 1924-
    The New Age movement / Philip H. Lochhaas.
p. cm.   — (How to respond series)
    Rev. ed. of: How to respond to— the New Age movement. 1989, © 1988.
    Includes bibliographical references.
    ISBN 0-7586-1627-9
    1. New Age movement—Controversial literature. I. Title. II. Series.

BP605.N48L63 1995
299'.93—dc20   95–8596

---

1 2 3 4 5 6 7 8 9 10   19 18 17 16 15 14 13 12 11 10

CONTENTS

1 **OLD LIES FOR A NEW AGE**   5

2 **A HISTORY OF, AND REASONS FOR, THE NEW AGE**   14

3 **NEW AGE OCCULTISM**   22

4 **NEW AGE HUMANISM**   37

5 **WHAT DOES THE BIBLE SAY?**   54

6 **A CHRISTIAN'S RESPONSE TO THE NEW AGE MOVEMENT**   59

RESOURCES   76

NOTES   77

1 OLD LIES FOR A NEW AGE

Beginning in the 1980s, the phrase *New Age* increasingly came to the attention of many people. However, the ideas and concepts of the New Age Movement have existed in one form or another for a long time. In fact, it has been around almost since the beginning of time. Its lies are as old as those of Satan in the Garden of Eden (see chapter 2). The impression that it is *new* has been created by the media, which often focus on its strange practices and overlook its philosophical or religious side.

The New Age Movement is a *movement*, a network of many organizations. Popular writers like Constance Cumbey, Texe Marrs, and M. Scott Peck made the New Age Movement appear to be widespread and organized. Sociologist Marilyn Ferguson, in her work *The Aquarian Conspiracy*, gives the impression that the New Age Movement is larger than it is.[1] On the other hand, among those involved in New Age ideas and practices, there is enough agreement to identify a specific and distinct belief system.

The New Age Movement may be defined as a network of otherwise dissimilar people intent on replacing the reality of a personal God with the idea that humanity is the center of all things. Indeed, some claim that each person is God, one with a universal energy, and only needs to develop the potential of divinity to the fullest. But no brief definition can explain the rapid spread of the movement in American society. This can be understood only by giving attention to the history of the movement as well as the basic principles of the New Age philosophy.

AN IMPORTANT DISTINCTION

The New Age Movement appears to be a confusing and contradictory mix—until one understands that there are two distinct expressions of the movement: there is the occult and there is the humanistic. The *occult* expression involves such ideas and practices as reincarnation, the power of crystals, channeling spirit guides, UFO phenomenon, and the worship of self. The *humanistic* expression focuses on developing unlimited human potential and an ethical system centered in responsibility only to one's self.

The occult expression of the New Age Movement attracts those interested in the latest fad. For that reason it is often dismissed as trivial. While the practice of some New Age fads—the use of crystals, sitting under a pyramid, looking for ways to contact personal guardian angels—may decrease, the occult New Age is not trivial. It has left behind a trail of spiritual death, and it continues to endure because of the great number of its participants.

The humanistic New Age Movement has been around ever since Satan convinced Adam and Eve that they could be God's equal. Down through the centuries, like a chameleon, it has changed its colors in order to blend into a new environment. Today it continues to promote Satan's agenda as it seeks to involve every social, cultural, and religious aspect of life in his deceptive lies. Since New Age humanism is synonymous with the fall of humanity, it will remain until Jesus comes again.

Because it attracts the sinful human nature and because of its subtle deceptiveness, the New Age Movement has become a major challenge to Christianity in

Referring to the New Age penetration into politics, Dr. Walter Martin of the Christian Research Institute wrote: "The New Age political agenda is dangerous because it completely ignores man's greatest problem—*sin*—as well as God's provision for this problem—the substitutionary atonement of Jesus Christ." (Walter Martin, *The New Age Cult* [Minneapolis: Bethany House, 1989], 74.)

our time. Both the occult and the humanistic expressions of the New Age Movement see themselves as offering "salvation" to humanity. New Age proponents identify salvation as personal enlightenment (transformation) to the divinity within. Such enlightenment will, in turn, lead to humanity's evolutionary leap into a new world order of peace and harmony.

It is easy to confuse the New Age philosophy with the secular humanism (deification of humanity) of the past. However, despite some similarities, the New Age Movement is not the same as modern secularism (the separation of church and state). Nor is it the same as Eastern mysticism. It borrows freely from both sources while also drawing Western occultism, humanistic psychology, ancient and medieval witchcraft, and pagan pantheism into the mix. It represents a relentless quest toward self-deification and the integration of all knowledge and spirituality to create a utopian society.

It is important for Christians to recognize that by replacing God with deified human beings, the New Age Movement is religious to the core and is fundamentally hostile to essential Christian beliefs. The Christian Church must not merely denounce the movement but also minister to the vacuum in people's lives on which the movement feeds.

THE NEW AGE PRINCIPLES

There are many branches off the occult and humanistic forks of the New Age tree, but six broad principles form the roots from which the New Age philosophy grows. The importance that various New Age entities attach to one or another of these principles will vary, but the principles in one form or another express a kind of New Age "creed." At the same time, the interpretation of and additions to the following six principles often separate humanistic and occult New Agers from one another.

1. *All is one; therefore all is God.* This principle expresses the twin concepts of *monism* and *pantheism*, which have long been identified with the Eastern religions. The New Age god is impersonal and does not exist distinct from creation. "It" is a universal energy, the Force, the combined consciousness, the oneness (monism) of all living things. In this oneness, good and evil, life and death, are the same. Differences exist only in perception.

If all is one, then this universal energy, this impersonal god, is in all things (pantheism). Jane Roberts, channeler of the spirit entity Seth and author of *The Seth Material* (Manhasset, NY: New Awareness Network, 2001), describes the New Age idea of God: "He is not one individual, but an energy gestalt . . . and because its energy is within and behind all universes, systems, and fields, it is indeed aware of each sparrow that falls, for it *is* each sparrow that falls."[2]

2. *Humanity, like all creation, is divine and has unlimited potential.* This New Age principle simply says that each person is God in disguise. Any human being may say, "I am God" in the same sense that "the man from Nazareth" said it. A related concept to the divinity of humanity is that, as God, each person creates his or her own reality. Since the divine energy will admit no limitations, human beings

"It is the basic tenet of pantheism, the core belief of Hinduism: All things are One, since all energy is divine consciousness 'frozen' into matter. . . . Man in his deepest self is none other than God. But without 'enlightenment,' he does not know this. . . . The purpose of man is to realize that he is God, thus ending the 'illusion' of separation." (Tal Brooke, *When the World Will Be as One* [Eugene, OR: Harvest House, 1989], 73.)

themselves have no limitations as they visualize and create their own reality. They can evolve into anything they choose. Being divine and creating their own reality, humans are under no law and accountable to none but themselves. There is no absolute apart from the reality of right and wrong each person creates.

10

3. *Humanity's basic flaw is its ignorance of divinity and oneness with all things.* The human race obviously has problems, but its major problem is not sin. The only barrier to humanity's further evolution is ignorance of its divinity, but ignorance can be dispelled by "enlightenment." Humanity's arrival at perfection comes through an evolutionary or awakening process called "transformation." Transformed humanity is the savior of humanity. We have personal and world problems because a critical mass of enlightened beings that will produce a total transformation of the human race has not yet been achieved.

4. *Humanity's only need, therefore, is transformation— the awareness of divinity.* We are our own creators and, therefore, responsible for everything that happens to us and around us. The capture and directing of our future evolution constitutes our only hope. Recognizing our divinity and choosing wisely the direction of humanity's evolution, we will achieve the betterment of humanity. Marilyn Ferguson finds support for the "evolutionary leap" of humanity in the theories of some scientists that the evolutionary process is punctuated by the sudden appearance of fully formed, highly evolved new species.[3]

5. *Transformation can be produced by a wide variety of techniques.* Each of these techniques seeks to induce an altered state of consciousness. The desired result is that a

person's current belief system (faith) will be replaced by a new perception of reality based on the belief that humanity is its own creator.

Marilyn Ferguson lists the following "systems for a deliberate change in consciousness": induced sensory isolation (e.g., flotation tank) or sensory overload, biofeedback, chanting, psychodrama, hypnosis and self-hypnosis, "meditation of every description" (especially the many forms of yoga), feverish dancing, magical rites, human potential seminars (e.g., Silva Mind Control, Lifespring), dream journals, primal therapy, "rebirthing," syncretistic religions (e.g., Theosophy), body disciplines (e.g., the martial arts), self-healing (e.g., Science of the Mind), *A Course in Miracles*, and more.[4]

Other New Agers would add to this list guided imagery and visualization, therapeutic touch, sleep deprivation, endurance tests, fire walking, pyramidology, use of crystals, astrology, and "channeling" of spirits. Almost anything is acceptable that will trigger a mystic or psychic experience powerful enough to cause a person to reject his or her former beliefs and perception of reality.

6. *Personal transformation is the springboard to global transformation.* The mark of such global transformation is mass enlightenment and global unity. According to

New Agers, further transformation of humanity will inevitably become universal, climaxing in a golden age that will be free of all war, violence, racism, disease, hunger, and death. Some believe that humanity will be truly "one," with one language, one monetary system, one world government, one religion, and one mind and will.

Syncretism in New Age terminology identifies the effort to create one world religion based on the idea that, at their core, all religions are one and teach the oneness of all things. In this system the exclusive claims of Christianity are denied, and the scriptural Christ is replaced with the idea of the "Christ-consciousness in you."

Some have even suggested that all people will think the same thoughts at the same time.

The highly touted "quantum leap" into divinity in a perfect world is just around the corner, according to many New Age promoters, and New Age philosophy is heavily promoted in popular culture. Like a commercial product, promoters package it attractively and advertise widely, often making use of endorsements by popular entertainers and other famous figures. When feeling a need for spiritual enlightenment, however, the individual needs to ask, "If I pursue a New Age teaching or technique, will I find myself dancing in the light or walking in darkness?"

13

2 A History of, and Reasons for, the New Age

Tracing the history and development of the New Age Movement can easily fill several volumes. It was conceived when four lies were devised by Satan to destroy the relationship of Adam and Eve with the Creator God and bring them under Satan's dominion: "You will not surely die . . . your eyes will be opened, . . . you will be like God . . . desired to make one wise" (Genesis 3:4–6). As mentioned in chapter 1, these same deceptions are repeated in some of the basic principles and teachings of the New Age Movement: human beings are like God—divine; humanity needs transformation; in the knowledge of one's divinity lies wisdom and power; and often, there is no death, only endless reincarnations.

These "New Age" ideas originating in the lies of Satan are traceable through continued repetitions in Old Testament times (Psalm 2) and in New Testament times (Romans 1:25). Already in the New Testament period

(John 1, Colossians 1–2) and during several centuries that followed, the Gnostic heresy represented an attempt to blend Christianity with older pantheism and pagan religions. The discovery of a divine spark within the self, the Gnostics said, enabled people to see a cosmic oneness that removed all limitations from the human being. Lutheran pastor Don Matzat observes in *Inner Healing*:

> While Protestant Christians accept the fact that there is no new truth, church history demonstrates that there is no new heresy either. The New Age Movement offers nothing new to this age. We are dealing with "the same ol' stuff in a different wrapper.[1]

The Gnostic heresy survived for centuries during the spread of Christianity, appearing in various forms. Its modern "New Age" revival can be traced to Madame Helena Blavatsky. In the latter half of the nineteenth century she founded the Theosophical Society, a blend of Eastern religion, occult speculation, and Gnostic interpretation of Christianity. Her prize pupil, Alice Bailey, developed Blavatsky's teachings into an organized system and coined the term *New Age*. Bailey taught that humanity must achieve enlightenment by realizing its divinity. Bailey's teachings are kept alive today by the

Gnosticism: an ancient heresy built on the concept of a duality of matter and spirit, with matter being evil and spirit being good. "Salvation," deliverance of the spirit from the captivity of the fleshly body, was accomplished by acquiring special wisdom or secret knowledge (Greek *gnosis*).

Lucis Trust and its political lobby, World Goodwill, as well as by many New Age writers.

The New Thought Movement constitutes another block in the New Age foundation. Its origins generally are traced to the mental healing practice of Phineas Parkhurst Quimby in the mid-nineteenth century. The Church of Christ, Scientist, founded by Mary Baker Eddy, has become one of the better-known developments of New Thought teachings. In her major work, *Science and Health with Key to the Scriptures*, Eddy writes, "There is no life, truth, intelligence, nor substance in matter. All is infinite Mind and its infinite manifestation, for God is All-in-all."[2] The parallels to the basic New Age principle "All is One; all is God" are obvious.

Thus, New Age spirituality cannot be traced to just one source (e.g., Eastern mysticism), as some have tried to do. It is a pick-and-choose blend of the primal human effort to replace God with self, pagan superstition, occult mysticism, and syncretistic religion. And there is one more ingredient: secular humanism.

Secular humanism, as set forth in *A Humanist Manifesto* (1933—hereafter cited as *Manifesto*) and *Humanist Manifesto II* (Buffalo, NY: Prometheus, 1973), found its support chiefly among educators and proponents of the human potential movement. "The traditional dualism of mind and body must be rejected" (*Manifesto I*, 8). "Human life has meaning because we create and develop our future" (*Manifesto II*, 17). The New Age Movement, by adding New Age spirituality, has adapted many similar ideas. Secular humanism and the New Age Movement coexist rather than compete, for in the final analysis, there is little difference between declaring that the human being is divine and maintaining that humans are the highest beings.

REASONS FOR THE NEW AGE'S POPULARITY TODAY

The reasons for the modern development of the ancient lies of the New Age are many and complex. They include scientific, cultural, social, and religious factors.

The New Age Movement represents a *rebellion against science and technology.* Many people are disenchanted about much of science today. Scientists and their technology continue to reshape the lives of millions of people. Yet the basic problems of day-to-day existence remain largely unsolved. The space-food-energy crises continue to increase around the world.

For many people, scientific solutions cannot deal adequately with these crises. Yet the only hope that many can envision comes from humanity. "Humans are responsible for what we are or will become. No deity will save us; we must save ourselves" (*Manifesto II*, 16). Humanity has the potential, they feel, to evolve further and reach perfection. To that end we must actively pursue a higher consciousness. That is the only hope for those who reject God, as has always been true when the Word of God goes unheeded. When calamity came on the Egyptians, they scurried about consulting idols, sorcerers, mediums (channelers), and necromancers (Isaiah 19:3).

The failure of secular humanism has contributed much to the rise of the New Age Movement. Ours is simply not a secular society. The religious impulse is a created part of human nature, a law written in the human heart (Romans 2:15). Our hearts are restless until they rest in God, said St. Augustine. G. K. Chesterton's observation has been quoted often: "When a man ceases to believe in God, he does not believe in nothing. He believes in anything." In times of national and international unrest, religious revival is quite common. The New Age Movement is, in a sense, such a religious revival. But it does not rescue humanity from the emptiness to which secular humanism inevitably leads. Instead, it offers a puny shout at the heavens: "I am God!" It is like the rooster on the manure pile who believes that his crowing causes the sun to rise each morning.

Churches have also contributed to the rise of the New Age Movement. Many mainline churches have become increasingly secularized. Some have eroded belief in the supernatural, in miracles, in God's provident and intervening power. Abandonment of the great moral imperatives of God's revealed Word has led to a crisis of values in many churches. The Ten Commandments have become "ten suggestions," expressed in psychological clichés and moral compromises. Add the glossy commercial packaging of television's Christian programming, and it is little wonder that spirituality has diminished in many churches. John C. Cooper minces no words:

> When you abandon the centrality of God's divine initiative—our unmerited election in Christ and the faith given us by God through the proclaiming,

A HISTORY OF, AND REASONS FOR, THE NEW AGE

loving activity of the one, holy, apostolic and catholic church—you are on the naked plains of the human spirit where any demon that comes along can consume you.[3]

America's love affair with the "quick fix," fast food for both soul and body, also contributes to the popularity of the New Age Movement. The New Age Movement offers easily available sensual experiences in place of analyzing problems and making tough decisions. Unlike self-discipline, the New Age does not make demands. A "fast food mentality" finds it easy to believe that problems accumulated over a lifetime can be solved in a weekend retreat.

But Satan's strategy, however, makes the greatest contributions to the New Age Movement's popularity. Throughout the

"Both [Bill] Alnor and [Keith] Tolbert [cult researchers] assert that many mainline churches have gutted themselves spiritually by denying the real Gospel. In so doing they have left a spiritual vacuum—'the main reason why so many mainline religions are adopting elements of the New Age,' says Tolbert." (Joe Maxwell, "Cult Watchers See Troubling Trends," *Christian Research Journal* [Spring/Summer 1994]: 42.)

thousands of years of human existence, Satan has had a single purpose: to dethrone God. He deceives human beings into believing that they possess God's attributes, thus rendering the atonement of Jesus Christ unnecessary. Satan would be a fool to abandon the "new" philosophy that has been so successful in all generations. He has been called by many names in Scripture, but "Fool" is not one of them.

3 NEW AGE OCCULTISM

Occult expressions of the New Age Movement accept the New Age principles quite literally and add specific beliefs of their own.

OCCULT BELIEFS

Belief in *reincarnation* and *karma* forms a vital part of the occult New Age. Recent surveys indicate that around 25 percent of the American population accepts reincarnation as an explanation of life after death.[1] Reincarnation is a basic doctrine of Hinduism. The westernized version of reincarnation expresses the belief that the immortal soul/spirit, the true inner self, passes from one human body to another in a continuous cycle of death and rebirth. Reincarnation assures New Agers they will live again when the evolutionary transformation of the human race finally reaches the "golden age" of global peace and harmony.

Karma, the balance of good and evil, is the controlling agent for each subsequent incarnation. Karma is the

Hindu law of cause and effect—good produces good and evil produces evil. Some New Agers speak of karma as the instrument by which each person *chooses* the experiences of his or her next life. In order to rid oneself of vast amounts of negative karma, a person may elect to be aborted or born handicapped, suffer from cancer, live in extreme poverty, etc. Russell Chandler writes, "Reincarnation American style meets psychological needs, attempting in the process to resolve the moral failures of life while hanging onto a hope for survival and salvation."[2]

The New Age teachings of reincarnation and karma sound the death knell of all social ministry. Who would dare to interfere with the law of karma by aiding those who have chosen their present state? Karma has no concept of forgiveness. Its absolute relentlessness requires that each person work off their karmic debt until they achieve godhood.

Belief in reincarnation leads to one of the most bizarre practices of the occult New Age: channeling spirit guides. Nineteenth-century mediums claimed to contact the spirits of deceased persons. Twentieth-century channelers claim to be human vehicles for higher spirit entities who currently have no physical existence on the earth plane.

These spirit entities are said to be extremely knowledge-able and desire to impart their advanced wisdom so that humanity might evolve to higher levels of consciousness. The spirit beings take various levels of control of their human channels in ways ranging from automatic writing to full-body and mind control while the channel is in a trance state.

"Spiritual channeling is the process of leaving . . . waking consciousness and becoming a conduit for a source of energy not normally in your awareness. You may have a sense of reaching . . . a spirit guide. Thoughts or images which are not your own may enter your mind; or you may find yourself speaking in a way that differs from your ordinary thought process." (Channels, Newsletter of The Center for Transformation, vol. 1:1 [Summer 1988].)

Channeled spirits may include a thirty-five thousand-year-old warrior, a six-year-old from Atlantis, Merlin of Camelot, a woman who will be born six hundred years in the future on Venus, dolphins ("they are *so* evolved!"), angels, and even Jesus (*A Course in Miracles*). From any other source their messages would be considered trite: "Love yourself" or "You deserve a good life." These clichés are laced with genuine New Age philosophy: "You are a divine being. . . . There is never any reason to feel guilt. . . . You create your own reality. . . . You have the power within your-self to be anything you choose." Channeling sessions can turn out to be more than just a diversion for the terminally bored. Tragedies have followed from the advice given by some channels.

The *use of crystals* has been an identifying feature of the occult New Age. Quartz crystals, one of the most naturally occurring substances in the earth's surface, are invested with powerful attributes, similar to ancient paganism assigned powerful magic to unusual or pretty rocks. New Age crystals supposedly channel energy for healing, power, and wisdom. Different colors of quartz affect different parts of the body, and the crystals can be "programmed" to meet particular needs. Crystals are taped to a carburetor to improve gasoline mileage, placed in drinking water to promote healing, or worn around the neck to increase energy and mind powers.

Extraterrestrials and UFOs also play an important role in occult New Age thinking. Distant star sys-tems are believed inhabited by highly cultured races that are spiritually and scientifically millions of years ahead of humans. These "intelligences from space" apparently share their advanced knowledge through specially chosen human mediators. Even if real, are these extraterrestrials interplanetary or interdimensional (demonic)? One would suspect the latter, for the message they bring consistently opposes Christian teaching.

Various divination practices also characterize the occult New Age. Insecure with life in the present, humanity has sought in every age to look into the future. New Age divination practices are, like much in the New Age Movement, really not new. They are simply adaptations of ancient, God-forbidden practices.

> There shall not be found among you anyone who burns his son or his daughter as an offering, anyone who practices divination or tells fortunes or interprets omens, or a sorcerer or a charmer or a medium or a necromancer or one who inquires of the dead, for whoever does these things is an abomination to the Lord. And because of these abominations the Lord your God is driving them out before you. (Deuteronomy 18:10–12)

Such divination practices intend to heighten psychic powers. Astrologers cast horoscopes claiming that part of God's creation (stars and planets) determine the destiny of another part of God's creation (humanity). Long-distance "900" numbers and Web sites are available for people to contact psychics who will, for a fee, provide psychic counseling ranging from advice for the lovelorn to financial planning. New Age diviners continue to promote Satan's old lie that humanity can be like God and know not only good and evil but also the future.

VEHICLES OF THE OCCULT NEW AGE

A variety of New Age events and happenings provides opportunities for participants to experience the rich diversity and consciousness-altering power of New Age spirituality. These events also attract publicity for the New Age Movement organizers and profiteers.

Mind, body, and spirit festivals (psychic fairs) are examples of such events. They have drawn as many as 100,000 New Agers and curiosity seekers to visit "experts" who will tell them about their previous lives, instruct them in astrology, numerology, tarot readings, crystal power, auras, and UFOs, and sell them pyramids, crystals, herbal remedies, flower essences, and health foods.

Occasionally, New Agers have attempted to involve people all over the world in "projecting their energies" at exactly the same instant in order to bring about world peace and prosperity. *The World Instant of Cooperation*, December 31, 1986, was promoted with the goals of bringing about a "planetary pentecost" by conferring godhood on humanity, eliminating all national boundaries, establishing one world religion, and arriving at immortality. In August 1987, a worldwide festival of *Harmonic Convergence* was held. A minimum of 144,000 "rainbow humans" were needed to gather at ancient sacred sites around the world in order to bring about a "resonant attunement" that would propel humanity into the New Age. All the baggage of occult expression was brought into play: pagan rituals, shamanistic rites, purifications, crystal power, and so forth.

In 1993, the *Parliament of World Religions* was held in Chicago (the first such gathering since 1893, but has now continued in 1999, 2004, 2007, and 2009 at different locations around the world). It demonstrated how "Eastern" the religions of the world have become, including some branches of Christianity. While not all religious faiths were well represented, the emphasis focused on Eastern and New Age concepts. "In effect, the event had the potential to move the vision of a world politically and spiritually united around New Age values and mysticism from the Western middle class to the world's religions at large."[3]

The entertainment industry must be seen as a primary vehicle for promoting occult New Age views. Films powerfully influence millions of minds. The *Star Wars* series was only the first among many films to make statements about a pantheistic "Force" that represents deity, intuitive communication with "the other side," and "ascended masters" that form a hierarchy for bringing humanity into the New Age. The *Matrix* trilogy, *The Golden Compass*, *Avatar*, and *2012* all promote the occult New Age philosophy. Even the immensely popular Disney movie series *The Lion King* contains overtones of New Age thinking. The oft-repeated message of these films is that people have all that they need within themselves and that the only reality is what is perceived.

Entrepreneurs appear to have the most to gain from the New Age Movement. People tend to be receptive to anything new, especially if it offers "experiences" in great quantity and variety. Publishers of New Age books are reaping an unimaginable bonanza. As of 2010, Amazon .com boasts over eighty-five thousand books categorized as New Age and fifty-five thousand categorized as occult. New Age shelves in general bookstores continue to expand. The number of stores devoted entirely to the sale of New Age books and artifacts continues to increase. Such shops sell astrological charts, crystals,

Margot Adler, priestess of a coven of witches, writes, "Divinity is immanent in all Nature. It is as much within you as without. . . . Women (and men too) will never understand their own creative strength and divine nature until they embrace the creative feminine, the source of inspiration, the Goddess within." (Margot Adler, *Drawing Down the Moon* [New York: Penguin, 1997], ix.)

pyramids, tarot cards, New Age music, as well as books on witchcraft, shamanism, creative visualization, and channeling. Weekend seminars for human potential and channeling can bring in four hundred dollars or more per attendee.

The occult New Age has also produced a revival of the neo-pagan goddess religion with its feminism that denies God as Creator. Occult New Agers point to a time in ancient history when the creation (the earth, moon, and stars) rather than the Creator was reverenced as an expression of female deity. That religion of the Great Mother goddess has been revived in opposition to Christianity, which is blamed for creating a male deity who delights in war and the exploitation of women and resources. The "Gaia Hypothesis" of New Age environmentalism regards the earth and all that it contains as a single living organism: feminine, self-creating, and self-nurturing.

Many names are associated with the occult expression of the New Age Movement. In the late 1980s and into the early 1990s, Shirley MacLaine, movie actress and dancer, ranked high in New Age visibility. Her several books and 1987 television miniseries made her name synonymous with the New Age Movement. MacLaine's bag of tools included mantras, crystals, a dogmatic reincarnation creed, and anything else that might be considered New Age. Her seminar lectures featured kundalini yoga, experiences in visualization, revelations regarding Lemuria (sister continent to mythical Atlantis), and sometimes even the rewriting of history.

In the New Age Movement, new names have become household words. J. Z. Knight, a Washington housewife, became a "guru to the stars," such as MacLaine and Linda Evans. Knight claimed to channel Ramtha, a thirty-five thousand year old warrior who gave revelations about the deity of humanity such as "God . . . has never been outside of you—it is you." Only those willing to pay four hundred dollars for a seminar may hear Ramtha speak "in person," but "his" books and CDs are sold widely.

Some surprising names are found among occult New Age devotees. Psychiatrist Elisabeth Kübler-Ross, whose

On Death and Dying is a standard textbook for college and hospital seminars, could not resist the lure of the occult. She began to dabble in spiritism and entered into the world of spirit guides and communications "from other planes of existence," much to the dismay of her former associates. In 2007, she was posthumously indicted into the National Women's Hall of Fame.

Barbara Marx Hubbard, once a respected futurist and a Democratic candidate for vice-president in 1984, also has become a New Age spokesperson. She helped organize and promote *The World Instant of Cooperation*. Hubbard expects a sudden and spectacular "quantum leap" in humanity's evolution in which a superhuman race would appear, a race as far superior to today's humanity as present humanity is to the apes. Along with other more philosophical New Agers, she has spoken of the necessity for some "selection process." By this she advocates that people who do not possess "God-consciousness" and are therefore incapable of further evolution be removed from the earth so that others may evolve unhampered by them.

Some have identified George Lucas as a "contemporary theologian" who, through his movies, has influenced people's ideas about God more than any other. Lucas produced the *Star Wars* and the *Indiana Jones* series as well as the movie *Willow*. The *Star Wars* series especially promotes the idea of an impersonal energy field, the Force, which surrounds each person and can be tapped for good or evil.

Former astronaut Edgar Mitchell is another surprising name found in the circle of occult New Agers. He appeared at former singer John Denver's (yet another prominent New Ager) New Age gatherings, which expressed concern over environmental issues. Mitchell is most often associated with his interest in UFO encounters and *A Course in Miracles*, a work its promoters claim was channeled by Jesus Christ through the atheistic Jew Helen Schucman. *A Course* sounds deceptively Christian and has been taught in Christian churches, often by Mitchell himself.

According to a foundation that promotes the distribution of *A Course*, a primary reason for the channeling of this three-volume work is to correct the errors of Christianity that, over the centuries, has supposedly misinterpreted the teachings of Jesus. Because of these errors, people have been led into misperceptions about the reality of sin, guilt, forgiveness, and the meaning of the crucifixion and resurrection of Jesus. The miracles of *A Course* are

"The aim of *A Course in Miracles* is to lead us from duality to one-ness—to the realization of our At-one-ment with God, our Self and all people—our brothers. . . . Salvation is really enlighten-ment, and enables us to accept the Christ within, and see with Christ's vision—love." Julius Finegold and William Thetford, eds., *Choose Once Again: Selections from* A Course in Miracles (Berkeley, CA: Celestial Arts, 1981), 3.

the corrections of these misperceptions in the minds of people. This occult work is a curious mix of theology in which humans are defined as sons of God in the same sense as Jesus, evil is overcome by perceiving things differently, and atonement is something humans do when they "revision reality."

Others not origi-nally associated with *A Course* have profited financially from it. In 1992, Marianne Williamson's *A Return to Love: Reflections on* A Course in Miracles reached the top of the *New York Times* best-seller list. She also made the rounds of the lec-ture circuit and was interviewed on the Oprah Winfrey show. Williamson's book, lectures, and interviews have further increased interest in *A Course*.

Several metaphysical organizations are enjoying a resur-gence of popularity due to the New Age Movement—the

34

Theosophical Society, Edgar Cayce's Association for Research and Enlightenment, the Ancient Mystical Order Rosae Crucis (AMORC), Unity School of Christianity, and Eckankar. The New Age Movement has also given birth to new organizations such as the Church of Religious Science, the Urantia Brotherhood (now reorganized as the Fifth Epochal Fellowship), the Church Universal and Triumphant, Transcendental Meditation, and the Inner Peace Movement.

In his book *The New Age Is Lying to You*, Eldon Winker writes,

> The occult aspect of the New Age demonstrates clearly that the old lies of Satan are still at work deceiving man into believing that he controls his eternal destiny. He and his demons disguise themselves as perfected beings of great intelligence whose only interest is to lead the human race to a self-achieved state of perfection. Many New Age tools become his instruments of spiritual destruction.[4]

THE TIMETABLE

New Age leaders agree that "the new order" (i.e., the Age of Aquarius) will arrive when a "critical mass" of individuals achieves "personal transformation." No one seems willing to define what constitutes a critical mass, but the theory compares to the proverbial "straw that broke the camel's back." At some time in the future the addition of just one more convert to the New Age Movement will trigger a universal consciousness shift, and humanity will have fully entered the New Age.

A fanciful and often highly embellished tale, "The Hundredth Monkey," is used by a number of New Age writers to illustrate how they expect critical mass theory to work. It deals with an island colony of monkeys, a number of which began to wash their food before eating. After one more monkey was added to ninety-nine that had adopted this custom over six years, suddenly all the monkeys began washing their food. New Agers have chosen various years as the New Age year of the hundredth monkey, but all predictions have obviously failed. In brief, the occult New Age sees humankind on the brink of omnipotence. Perfected beings who have achieved deity already walk among us, though unseen. Their powers and counsel are presently available to the "enlightened" who are willing to reject all objective truth and reality and enter the shadow world of self-deification.

4 NEW AGE HUMANISM

In chapter 1 it is stated that the New Age Movement consists of two movements in one: the occult and the humanistic. In chapter 3, we summarized the occult movement. In this chapter we will focus on the humanistic aspect of the New Age. Gone are the pagan superstitions, the magical devices, and the dreams of endless reincarnations—at least to the degree that these are a part of the occult expression. But the humanistic expression still includes the human-centered dreams for a perfect utopian society and world order.

Humanist New Agers acknowledge the two movements within the New Age Movement. New Ager David Spangler wrote an introductory essay for *The New Age Catalogue*, published by the editors of *Body, Mind & Spirit* magazine. In his essay, Spangler deplores the fact that the New Age often is identified with pagan religion, the occult, channeling, crystals, and reincarnation, which he calls a "limited and potentially distorting approach." He defines the New Age as "a rebirth of our sense of the sacred, an inner impulse to understand and *express our own divinity* in cocreation and synergy *with the divinity within creation* and with the Source of that divinity whose ultimate nature we are still seeking to know."[1]

At first glance, it appears that New Age humanism merely restates the old *secular* humanism. The same six principles seem to be found in each (see chapter 1). Yet there are also marked differences between them.

SIMILARITIES BETWEEN SECULAR AND NEW AGE HUMANISM

The tenets of secular humanism are identified most clearly in *Humanist Manifestos I & II* (see chapter 2). Excerpts from these may be compared to the six principles of the New Age Movement.

New Agers hold that God is an impersonal force, a universal energy, not distinct or separate from creation. Furthermore, humanity continually evolves toward a higher being or consciousness. *Manifesto I* declares, "[We] regard the universe as self-existing and not created. . . . Man . . . has emerged as the result of a continuous process" (pg. 8).

"Humanity is divine," the New Age principles state, and *Manifesto II* asserts, "No deity will save us; we must

38

save ourselves" (p. 16). In other words, no deity or divinity exists apart from humanity's full potential to solve the problems and complexities of human existence.

New Agers fault ignorance of inherent divinity as the cause for all human crises. The *Manifestos* blame an emphasis on divinity external to mankind: "We consider the religious forms and ideas of our fathers to be no longer adequate. . . . Traditional dogmatic and authoritarian religions that place revelation, God, ritual, or creed above human needs and experiences do disservice to the human species" (pp. 10, 15–16).

"Humanity needs transformation" is the watchword of the New Age Movement. *Manifesto I* uses "complete realization" to describe the same goal: "The complete realization of the human personality is considered to be the end of man's life" (p. 9).

The New Age Movement attaches more importance to the techniques by which transformation may be achieved. The *Manifestos* offer a simpler technique for transformation: "The humanist finds his religious emotions expressed in a heightened sense of personal life and in a cooperative effort to promote social well-being" (p. 9). "Technology is a vital key to human progress and development" (p. 22).

Finally, New Agers expect the "transformation" of a sufficient number of individuals to usher in a "global transformation" that will produce a perfect world order. Secular humanism is no less ambitious: "Man is at last becoming aware that he alone is responsible for the realization of the world of his dreams, that he has within himself the power for its achievement" (*Manifestos*, 10). "The next century can and should be the humanist century" (p. 14).

Neither secular nor New Age humanists accept any universal standards of morality or ethics. The secular humanist sees all ethics as "autonomous and situational" (p. 17), while the New Age humanist makes right and wrong a matter of "creating your own reality" in a given situation.

DIFFERENCES BETWEEN SECULAR AND NEW AGE HUMANISM

Despite many similarities, profound differences exist between secular and New Age humanism. The New Age humanist believes that ultimately humanity is God. Secular humanism does not overtly deny the existence of God but declares that belief in God is irrelevant to human needs in society. It urges maximum development of human potential but does not assert that human potential is unlimited or that human beings will arrive at deity.

Nothing in the above paragraph intends to defend secular humanism. Such secularism is an attack on God and His gracious providence. It is a denial of His powerful acts in history and His moral standards by which society can prosper. Above all, it rejects His grace in meeting humanity's foremost need for restoration of the relationship with God that existed at creation—through forgiveness in Jesus Christ (see the next chapter).

This comparison demonstrates that New Age humanism is a blatantly anti-God philosophy. It desires to replace God with humanity and to instill the belief that the attributes of God rightfully belong to human beings. To that end the New Age Movement is making a coordinated effort to enlist the basic structures of society in its quest for a deified humanity. The vehicles used to draw all areas of life under its discipline further define New Age humanism.

VEHICLES OF NEW AGE HUMANISM

In 1980, sociologist Marilyn Ferguson wrote *The Aquarian Conspiracy*, a volume that became definitive of the New Age philosophy. Already at that time she reported that more New Agers—tens of thousands of

"The New Age in public education: The deliberate use of consciousness-expanding techniques in education, only recently well under way, is new in mass schooling. . . . Altered states of consciousness are taken seriously: 'centering' exercises, meditation, relaxation, and fantasy are used to keep the intuitive pathways open and the whole brain learning."
(Marilyn Ferguson, *The Aquarian Conspiracy* [New York: Penguin, 2009], 295, 315).

them—were involved in public education than in any other line of work. She refers to those educators who try to bring change to the old structure as the "heroes of education." She quotes one of the "heroes" who said, "The psychology of becoming must be smuggled into the schools" (p. 281). Humanist New Age goals in elementary education were clearly expressed by Dr. C. M. Pierce, professor of education at Harvard University, in a speech to one thousand teachers at a seminar on childhood education in 1973:

> Every child in America entering school at the age of five is mentally ill, because he comes to school with certain allegiances toward our founding fathers, toward our elected officials, toward his parents, toward a belief in a supernatural Being, toward the sovereignty of this nation as a

separate entity. It is up to you teachers to make all of these sick children well by creating the international children of the future.[2]

One prominent and influential educator, Dr. Beverly Galyean (d. 1984), carried Dr. Pierce's philosophy of education even further into the New Age. Although somewhat dated now, her system of "confluent education" illustrates how the New Age philosophy has infiltrated public education. Despite its obvious religious content, the curriculum was introduced into thirty-eight public school districts in southern California. It used guided imagery, yoga, and biofeedback "to introduce the children to the Inner Self—the self that can guide them in making decisions or in knowing what is true and good." Galyean's educational philosophy is clearly stated in her own words in a frequently quoted summary that she supplied:

Once we begin to see that we are all God, that *we have the attributes of God,* then I think *the whole purpose of human life is to reown the Godlikeness within us*: the perfect love, the perfect wisdom, the perfect understanding, the perfect intelligence, and when we do that, we create back to that old, that essential oneness which is consciousness.[3]

A familiar adage declares that "a half-truth is more dangerous than a lie." Much of what is promoted by New Age humanism fits that description well. The teaching of "values clarification" is a case in point. Values clarification in itself is a necessary part of our daily existence. We clarify our values every time we make a choice—we consider the pros and cons, we weigh the alternatives, we compare the advantages and disadvantages of our options. No wise decision can be made without such a process. But choices are only made validly when they are measured by some standard, be it religious, moral, or cultural. Clarification of values without a standard by which to measure can rapidly lead to anarchy. In line with Galyean's philosophy of education, most of the values clarification taught in schools carries the understanding that no measuring standard may be imposed by teachers, parents, society, or the church—or even by scientific disciplines—because all truth is what the individual perceives to be true for him or her.

Father Maury Smith is committed to the use of the values clarification methodology. In his book *A Practical Guide to Value Clarification*, Smith comments on the Puritan and Victorian morality of our past. He writes:

> Value clarification as a methodology considers
> this moralistic stance to be an imposition upon the

individual of predetermined values, and it seeks instead a method whereby individuals can discover their own values. Thus, value clarification does not tell a person what his values should be or what values he should live by; it simply provides the means for him to discover what values he does live by.[4]

Smith's book also includes readings from a variety of other value clarification literature. One reading, "The Clarifying Response," indicates that in reply to a student's comment or judgment, the teacher's response is to be value free: "The clarifying response avoids moralizing, criticizing, giving values, or evaluating. The adult excludes all hints of 'good' or 'right' or 'acceptable,' or their opposites, in such responses."[5]

The New Age Movement widely influences the field of *psychology* through such individuals as Dr. Jean Houston and Marilyn Ferguson. Both have impressive credentials and are known as extraordinarily magnetic and effective public speakers. Dr. Houston has the gift of modifying her messages to match the expectancies of her audiences. In one radio interview in Houston she said, "The moral mandates, the structured givens that were laid down 2,000 years ago—they've run out. The story doesn't work."

Marilyn Ferguson began to make a name for herself as the publisher of the *Brain-Mind Bulletin*. In her book *The Aquarian Conspiracy*, from which we have already quoted several times, Ferguson writes:

> Someone is always trying to summon us back to a dead allegiance: Back to God, the simple-minded religion of an earlier day. "Back to the basics," simple-minded education. Back to simple-minded patriotism. And now we are being called back to simple-minded "rationality" contradicted by personal experience and frontier science.[6]

Ms. Ferguson's "personal experience and frontier science" is a meaningless generalization intended to sound factual and is contradicted by the "experience" of respected scientists on the "frontier."

Western respect for science has made it important for New Age physicists to seek acceptance of their beliefs by the general public. By using New Age thought along with scientific discovery, they have gained another avenue for injecting New Age philosophy into our society. Our culture once trusted the dedicated scientist as being unaffected by superstition and personal bias. But more and more often, scientists move between scientific fact and New Age philosophy. One example of this is New

Age physicist Fritjof Capra (*The Tao of Physics* [Berkeley, CA: Random House, 1975]) who moves back and forth between physics and metaphysics without distinction. It is interesting to note that Dr. Capra admits to having had a "psychic conversion" prior to his "scientific" discoveries. Many of his assertions are more properly mystic "revelations" than verifiable scientific conclusions. Another example is complexity theorist Stuart Kauffman. In his book, *Reinventing the Sacred* (New York: Basic Books, 2008), he attempts to identify acts of creativity, meaning, and purposeful action in the natural as the source of a natural god.

In 1993, The Reader's Digest Association produced *Family Guide to Natural Medicine*. By inclusion, early printings of the book give approval to such New Age alternative medicines as shamanistic healing, balancing yin and yang, therapeutic touch, yoga, reflexology, and any other such practice that "clears blockage in the body's flow of vital energy" ([Pleasantville, NY: Reader's Digest Association, 1993], p. 171).

The New Age has made significant inroads into the field of health care. Sensitive and conscientious physicians have for centuries declared that health is a matter of soundness of body, mind, and spirit. Now many New Age

47

health workers and healers have presumed to "discover" holistic health and have branded traditional medicine "depersonalized" and "drug oriented." New Age health care has especially found a place in nursing with the promotion of "therapeutic touch," a trance-state technique of moving one's hands about a patient's body in order to focus the Hindu *prana* or "universal life force" to promote healing. In some areas, state and federal funds have been used for training in this overtly religious ritual.

The New Age Movement has also entered national and international politics with great gusto. New Agers often take credit for raising concerns already raised by Christians and other non-New Agers: ecological pollution, energy depletion, economic injustice, nuclear threat, exploitation of people, and so on. These concerns are not the exclusive province of the New Age pantheistic belief in the divinity of created things.

The New Age Movement tries to make political gains while public attention is diverted by reports of the bizarre antics of a few high-profile New Age occultists. The Green Party of Western Europe is avowedly New Age and has succeeded in getting candidates elected to office. The party has a number of valid concerns, but it also endorses abortion and the homosexuality. Above

48

all, the Green Party rejects belief in a Creator God who is separate and distinct from a finite, created world. The American Green Party has not achieved the success of the European party but has had candidates on the ballot in various state elections.

On the international political scene, the United Nations has supplied a platform for New Age promoters through supporting or otherwise abetting New Age organizations such as Planetary Citizens. Founded by Donald Keys, a longtime UN consultant, its headquarters were once housed in the UN building. Robert Muller, a retired assistant secretary-general of the UN, is a New Age activist who believes the UN will play an important role in global transformation. In his book, *New Genesis*, Muller writes, "In us humans there are divine cosmic elements which will flower to the point that . . . the universe will become conscious in ourselves. . . . The incarnated God, or Christ, is in all of us and for all of us to manifest."[7]

NEW AGE CORPORATE SEMINARS

Promoters have found a wide market for the New Age philosophy among corporations. A variety of motivational and stress-management seminars promise personal transformation of employees—a spiritual "awakening" that will tap into an organizational "synergy" throughout the company. Synergy is one of the buzzwords of the humanistic New Age. Synergy uses Eastern language about an all-pervading, monistic deity to express the connection between employees that enables the company to harness their full potential. A surprising number of America's largest corporations have become involved in these New Age seminars, and until recently some have made attendance a condition of employment or job advancement.

A word of caution is necessary: Not all motivational and stress-management seminars are New Age. Many sound programs designed to help people recognize and further develop their latent talents and abilities certainly exist. Such programs are not per se contrary to Christian teachings. In fact, many of them can be seen as exercises in Christian stewardship. But a program is spiritually deceptive when it declares that human potential is unlimited (an attribute of God alone), that a person's only responsibility is to self, that reality is created by what is visualized or perceived, that no standards apply except those that people choose for themselves. Such spiritual deception identifies the occult or humanist bent of New Age seminars.

Some participants in New Age seminars have found the following principles offensive to their beliefs and intrusive in their lives:

1. Truth is what we perceive reality to be in our minds.
2. Traditional beliefs have become barriers to the full development of the human being.
3. If you don't have New Age thinking, you are depriving your employees and your corporation of your full potential.
4. To grow, you must change your attitudes, habits, and belief systems.
5. Self-esteem is the most important aspect of your life.
6. Universal knowledge exists and can be accessed through ESP.
7. You are your own judge and jury; set yourself free.
8. As long as we are inside our comfort zone, we don't have to walk a straight line morally to be free of anxiety or tension.

The final dogmatic statement above (8) is a good example of New Age philosophy. It erases all standards of right and wrong. Wrong is only whatever causes stress or tension. "Wrongness" is "being outside your comfort zone." The solution? Not the refusal to participate in what one formerly believed to be wrong, but "enlightenment," expansion of your comfort zone. And wrong becomes right.

One of the most common techniques used to "develop unlimited potential" in self-help business seminars is "visualization." This is the New Age practice of creating mental images that become realities, since reality is only perception. "Affirmations" play an important role in New Age visualization. They call for repetition of a desired outcome until it can be visualized successfully and thus realized. Once more, a half-truth is distorted into a deception. True, one cannot accomplish something that cannot be visualized, nor can one prosper in something that is not affirmed; but visualization is not the same as reality, and truth is not the same as affirmation.

Physical tests used by some New Age seminars are intended to overcome one's fears and provide a sense of exhilaration, even omnipotence, when completed. Some seminars use confrontational situations to break down a person's inhibitions. Others have lectures on how to set one's own moral standards. Some seminar sessions are devoted to meditation, self-hypnosis, or chanting.

In 1988, the federal Equal Employment Opportunity Commission ruled that employers must accommodate workers who, on religious grounds, object to required attendance at New Age seminars. The ruling was prompted by several lawsuits against employers concerning training programs that promoted religious and moral values quite different from those held by people required to attend.

New Age humanism can be summarized in a few sentences:

Richard Watring, the former personnel director for Budget Rent-a-Car Systems in Chicago: "I'm concerned that even strong Christians will look at this training and see nothing wrong with it. . . . I think it's the church's respon-sibility to assist the flock in the formation of a Christian world view so that they will be able to recognize a coun-terfeit belief system for what it is when it's looking them in the face" (*Christianity Today* [June 17, 1988]: 74).

1. There is no deity but humanity. Humanity is good.
2. Inherent in the individual are the right values.
3. Humanity evolves toward greater good.
4. Evil is a misperception of reality.
5. All value judgments are wrong, for everything is relative.
6. Change is always good.
7. The pursuit of humani-ty's destiny will inevitably solve all problems.

5 WHAT DOES THE BIBLE SAY?

The idea that there is anything "new" about the "New Age" Movement is quickly laid to rest by the Holy Scriptures: "What has been is what will be, and what has been done is what will be done, and there is nothing new under the sun. . . . It has been already in the ages before us" (Ecclesiastes 1:9–10). "What has been . . . before us" takes us back to humanity's beginnings. We have already considered how the basic principles of the New Age philosophy parallel the four deceptive lies Satan used with Adam and Eve (chapter 2). Thus began the age called "new" in our generation.

In contrast to the New Age principles, the Word of God repeatedly pronounces judgment on all who refuse to distinguish between Creator and creature. Severe judgment falls on the person who considers himself or herself divine. Repeatedly in Isaiah 43–45 God declares, "I am the Lord, and there is no other" (Isaiah 45:5). In Isaiah 47 the consequences of humanity's aspiring to divinity are given with this judgment: "[They] shall come upon you in full measure, in spite of your many sorceries and the great power of your enchantments. You felt secure in your wickedness, you said, "No one sees me"; your wisdom and your knowledge led you astray, and you said in your heart, 'I am, and there is no one besides me' " (Isaiah 47:9–10).

The prophet Ezekiel sharply reproves those who claim divinity: "Thus says the Lord God: 'Because your heart is proud, and you have said, "I am a god, I sit in the seat of the gods, in the heart of the seas," yet you are but a man, and no god, though you make your heart like the heart of a god' " (Ezekiel 28:1–2). The sharp distinction between the Creator and humanity is maintained throughout the Bible. The apostle Paul describes God as follows: "[God] who is the blessed and only Sovereign, the King of kings and Lord of lords, who alone has immortality, who dwells in unapproachable light, whom no one has ever seen or can see. To Him be honor and eternal dominion. Amen" (1 Timothy 6:15–16).

Indeed, refusal to distinguish between the Creator and creation not only brought on the fall into sin but is today responsible for every deplorable condition found in human society. Romans 1:18–32 leaves no doubt about the accelerating degradation that follows the deification of creation. The poet Virgil wrote, "We make our destiny by our choice of gods." We are shaped by what we worship. And worship of self lies behind the "depraved mind" that expresses itself in "dishonorable passions. . . . all manner of unrighteousness, evil, covetousness, malice" (Romans 1:26, 29). The evils described in Romans 1 are identical to the forces that brought down the classical ages of Greece and Rome and the "Force" that New Age philosophy would release on humanity.

TRANSFORMATION IS NEEDED

The Bible makes it quite clear that humanity needs transformation, but it must be an act of the grace of God—conversion—the beginning of a continuing transformation effected by God's Holy Spirit: "I appeal to you therefore, brothers, *by the mercies of God*, to present your bodies as a living sacrifice, holy and acceptable to God, which is your spiritual worship. Do not be conformed to this world, but be transformed by the renewal of your mind, that by testing you may discern what is the will of God, what is good and acceptable and perfect" (Romans 12:1–2; emphasis added).

Paul makes it quite clear that humanity's crises are not due to lack of consciousness-raising techniques: "All have sinned and fall short of the glory of God" (Romans 3:23). The crisis is humanity's relationship to God. Using "psychotechnologies" to alter one's consciousness cannot relieve it. God initiates healing through the redemption in Jesus Christ, and this healing is applied individually and personally by the gracious action of God's Holy Spirit. Only forgiveness accomplished in the atoning work of Jesus Christ bridges the chasm of sin that separates people from the abundant life that God intends for them.

THE NEW AGE MOVEMENT—A CONSPIRACY?

The rapid growth and pervasiveness of the New Age Movement in so many disciplines has caused some to conclude that some kind of master plot has been carefully orchestrated to take over the world (see chapter 1). New Age "conspiracy theories" should be viewed with caution, for they often prevent a rational assessment of the situation. New Agers differ greatly in their strategies to implement their ideologies.

Marilyn Ferguson speaks of "the Aquarian Conspiracy" but uses the term to describe a networking of otherwise unlike New Age entities working together to "transform every aspect of contemporary life." She calls for New Agers to spread their message in classrooms; through the media and the arts; in casual conversations at coffee

Scripture References

1. All is not one: Psalm 148; all is not God: Colossians 1:15–17.

2. Human beings are not God: Deuteronomy 32:29; Isaiah 45:5–6.

3. Humanity's crises stem not from ignorance but from sin: Ecclesiastes 7:20; Matthew 15:19.

4. Humanity does need to be "enlightened" to sin and grace: Matthew 4:16; 1 John 1:7; 2 Corinthians 5:17–21.

breaks, at parties, and in government offices; through lectures and seminars; and "in the guise of health books and sports manuals, in advice on diet, business management, self-assertion."[1]

A "conspiracy" there is—but it is not of human origin. Its roots are in Satan's attempt to dethrone God and obstruct the atonement of Jesus Christ— an attempt doomed to failure, for the works of Satan have already been judged (Luke 10:18; John 16:11; 1 John 3:8).

6 A Christian's Response to the New Age Movement

A Christian's response to the New Age Movement consists of three parts:

1. A personal knowledge of truth
2. A ministry to people
3. Bringing the Gospel of Jesus Christ to those who walk in darkness (the joy of evangelism)

PERSONAL KNOWLEDGE OF TRUTH

Christians do not depend on self-directed evolution to find fulfillment in their lives. They know that to be all they were created to be, they must have a living relationship with the Creator. Knowledge of the infinite Creator does not come from within finite creatures. It is revealed only by the Creator—in Jesus Christ and in the Holy Scriptures. Only by God's revelation and the gracious action of His

Holy Spirit can people know that the Creator God is a God of love, who has not forsaken humanity in spite of our attempts to replace God with self. In Jesus Christ, His only-begotten Son, God has reconciled us to Himself for time and for eternity.

This does not mean that Christians emerge victorious in every temptation and trial. They make no claim to perfection or even to being "good." Living in a world distorted by rebellion against God, Christians recognize that they live in a tension of not having "already been made perfect," yet pressing on "because Christ Jesus has made me His own" (Philippians 3:12). They remain vulnerable to the temptations of Satan while being assured of forgiveness in Jesus Christ. Too often the world caricatures Christians as men and women who think of themselves as superior to all others. There is no room for pride or arrogance for the Christian who in every condition of life must confess, "But for the grace of God . . ."

The Word of God, the Bible, is the source of spiritual life and the standard by which all spiritual teachings must be measured. Proponents of the New Age Movement can be very deceptive in the use of language. Some New Agers plainly state their beliefs in the divinity of humanity in direct anti-God language. Others cleverly disguise their beliefs by using Christian terminology with hidden New Age meaning. For example, many New Agers would agree that "Jesus is the Christ" but in an entirely different sense than that used in the Bible.

New Agers cannot ignore the influence that the teachings and the person of Jesus of Nazareth have had

"There is good reason for the great antipathy toward the historic Christ . . . in the New Age. Jesus simply defies all their categories and humbles all their works. . . . [He] was not just an extraordinarily good person . . . indwelt by the Christ or Cosmic Consciousness, as the New Age proclaims. He is the King of kings and the Lord of lords. . . . No one comes to the Father but by Him (John 14:6)" (Walter Martin, *The New Age Cult* [Minneapolis: Bethany House, 1989], 39).

on Western culture. They must include Him near or at the top of their list of avatars or ascended masters. Therefore, the New Age Movement highly respects Jesus, but not as the Christ of Scripture. The Christ of the New Age Movement is only one of many "divine personages" who have appeared through the centuries. His mission, like that of other great teachers of the past as well as of New Agers today, was to awaken the masses to their own divinity.

New Age distortions of truth extend beyond the Bible, hence Christians must also diligently pursue truth and be alert for falsifications of history. For example, assertions that ancient Egyptians believed in reincarnation are totally contrary to fact. Not only are references to reincarnation absent from the ancient records, but the burial practices of the Egyptians were predicated on their belief that the dead would not return again to live on earth.

Of more serious consequence is the assertion that reincarnation was taught in the Bible and the Early Church until Justinian banned such teaching in AD 553 at the Second Council of Constantinople. Others blame the emperor Constantine at the Council of Nicaea. The Early Church Fathers were aware of reincarnation as a pagan belief ("one of the fabulous doctrines of the heathen"—Gregory of Nyssa, 335), but it was obviously not a "censored" Bible that the fathers quoted. Origen, sometimes cited by New Agers as a reincarnationist, wrote a lengthy refutation of such teaching, declaring, "We do not find this at all in the Divine Scriptures." Yet New Age writers repeat these erroneous assertions over and over again, until their statements appear to be fact.

Deception is also found in the occult New Age's touting of belief in reincarnation as a *teaching of hope*. A tour of the cities of India where the "New" Age has held people in thrall for centuries will reveal the starvation, poverty, disease, exploitation, and utter hopelessness that have resulted from the relentless laws of karma, reincarnation, and the self-deifying worldview. Is this the "final evolutionary leap," the "golden age" to which the New Age Movement would bring all humanity?

Christians need clear discernment, even as certain cautions are observed. What is New Age and what only appears to be (because of similarities of language, etc.) must be carefully distinguished. Broad assumptions serve no good purpose. The "New Age" label cannot be attached to everything that encourages self-improvement, mental discipline, a global perspective on humanity's problems, or healthy and organic eating. Not every person who uses phrases or buzzwords favored by the New Age Movement can be presumed to be a part of it. Hasty conclusions must not be drawn on the basis of language alone; a larger interpretive context is required to positively identify New Age thought.

It should also be noted that though many corporate motivational seminars teach New Age principles under the guise of developing human potential, not all personal growth seminars are New Age. Many seminars can be beneficial to the Christian's personal and professional growth. Such seminars may teach freedom from irrational fears and self-defeating negative views, personal discovery through testing and experience, and affirmation of the worth of every individual, including the aged, diseased, unprotected, and unwanted.

Some New Age critics charge the "Positive Confession" or "Word/Faith" teachers within Christianity with being New Age. While some parallels between the "success" preachers and New Age spokespersons do exist, there is a vast difference between misapplication of the Gospel of Jesus Christ and an outright denial of it. Some "success" preachers border on New Age thinking when they present the Gospel as a formula for manipulating God into providing perfect health, unlimited wealth, and success in every undertaking. This "theology of glory" does violence to the Word of God by drawing attention away from the centrality of the cross of Jesus Christ, but it is not New Age denial of the God who is Creator, Redeemer, and Sanctifier.

CONFESSING CHRIST AS REDEEMER

Christians do not seek merely to save the world from New Age philosophy. Rather, they seek to minister to all who knowingly or unknowingly share a common Creator and Redeemer.

Confessing, or witnessing, Christ to people, including those in the New Age Movement and those attracted to it, begins by recognizing the problems of great magnitude facing the world today: war, crime, poverty, hunger, racism, and depletion of resources. No human being, Christian or New Ager, should be so preoccupied with self that responsibility for addressing these problems should be left to others. While sharing many of these concerns with New Agers, Christians also feel a special responsibility. As stewards created to have dominion over the earth to the glory of God (Genesis 1:28; 9:1–7), Christian people should actively develop social, economic, and ecological programs that reflect the divine mandate to seek the good of all people. At the same time, the differences between Christian and New Age worldviews must be clearly defined.

Christians and non-Christians live amid the stress-producing complexities and changes of modern life. Both personal and world problems must be faced. The insights of modern psychology and psychiatry, as long as they do not contradict God's Word, can assist with personal problems. Working through difficult situations provides

Christians the opportunity to testify to the power of faith in Jesus Christ, to point to the true Gospel. In any case, the supportive ministry of fellow strugglers is vitally important for the warmth and acceptance it brings.

All human beings desire confirmation of their personal worth. Our God has attached such great personal worth to every individual that He did not spare His own Son to redeem humanity from the folly of its broken relationship with Him as Creator and Lord of all. The wonder of God's love is that *"while we were still sinners, Christ died for us"* (Romans 5:8; emphasis added). As Christ's disciples, Christians must regard every person as the object of God's redeeming love: the aged, the diseased, the nonproductive, the unwanted, and especially the unprotected (e.g., the unborn who cannot speak for themselves). Christians do not believe that realizing human potential is anti-Christian. At the same time they must not allow self-esteem to take the place of God-esteem as the measure of human worth.

God calls Christians to be His people in everything they do. The Christian life cannot be fragmented into religious, family, business, community, recreational, and personal segments. In every walk of life, Christians are to "shine as lights in the world, holding fast to the word of life"

(Philippians 2:15–16). A moral standard drawn from the Word of God and applied without reservation to every circumstance of life provides the Christian's guide. Faith must act on behalf of others: forgiving the erring, raising the fallen, and encouraging the victorious. Christian compassion can find many areas for serving: taking a stand on moral issues, writing letters to support people who demonstrate a strong moral position, contributing and volunteering services to moral causes and agencies of mercy, and running for public office. Douglas Groothuis makes a strong point in *Unmasking the New Age*:

> Christianity is a full-orbed world and life view. . . . It must implement the truth into all areas of life and thought. If Christians abandon crucial aspects of culture—education, politics, science, psychology, health, and others—counterfeit philosophies will . . . fill the void. Because this has happened in the recent past, Christians are partially responsible for the rise of the New Age. When and where Christians retreat, the enemy advances.[1]

The Christian life that demonstrates the love of God is often the first step toward gaining an audience for the proclamation of the Gospel of Jesus Christ.

THE JOY OF EVANGELISM

Although demonstration of Christian compassion and the confirmation of the worth of every individual are Christian imperatives, they do not substitute for proclamation of the Christian Gospel. Those who follow the "pied piper" of the New Age philosophy must be confronted with the Gospel of the God who loves them enough to die for them in Jesus Christ. This Good News must be verbalized in clear and forceful language. We testify to what God has done. The way of salvation is not humans aspiring to be God, but God becoming human and dying in our stead for the sins we have committed against Him. We find our true selves when we look away from ourselves to our Creator, Redeemer, and Sanctifier. But will the New Ager who shouts into the darkness "I am God" be likely to see the need for healing in Jesus Christ? Never sell God's Holy Spirit short!

To some the New Age Movement appears to be a fad that will quickly pass from the contemporary scene and therefore hardly worth special Christian concern. Nothing could be further from the truth. It is the latest and most blatant expression of humanity's rebellion against God. Although the name of the rebellion may change from time to time, it will continue as long as the world stands.

Others feel that New Agers are so committed to their beliefs that they will not even hear the Gospel when it is spoken. That, too, is far from true. Many New Age adherents are quite uncertain about what to believe. They quickly move from one practice or teaching to another, continually searching, grasping at any straw that promises to keep them afloat. New Agers know there is something wrong with humanity. While they are at a loss to explain what it is, they know some kind of transformation must happen if humanity is to live in harmony with itself and its environment.

In *The Aquarian Conspiracy*, Marilyn Ferguson admits that "the escalating crisis is a symptom of our essential wrongheadedness."[2] The keyword here is "essential." Our "wrongheadedness" requires more than a mere change in consciousness or adoption of a new worldview. It is symptomatic of humanity's rejection of the Creator and Source of life.

It must be understood that evangelism is not entering into debate over personalities of New Age leaders or the destructive social effects of New Age philosophy. Evangelism does not quarrel over who is "right" and who is "wrong." The essence of evangelism is telling the Good News about Jesus Christ—His life, suffering, death, and resurrection—by which God has accomplished the forgiveness of sins and reconciled a world of sinners to Himself. The Holy Spirit takes the responsibility for getting the results; our calling is to share the Gospel with those who do not yet confess Jesus Christ as Lord.

What "tools" can we use to meet the spiritually destructive claims of the New Age Movement? Too often we cast about for new weapons to combat what we perceive to be new threats to our beliefs. There are no "new" tools or weapons, and none are needed. We meet the New Age Movement in the same way we meet every spiritual deception: armed with the Word of God. The Bible is an anvil that has worn out many a hammer that has beat against it, and it proves as effective against error today as it has ever been.

The Word must be used, however, with an awareness of the hungers that the New Age Movement tries to fill. These vary considerably from one individual to another. Hence no sure-fire method or approach for reaching every New Ager exists. Some suggestions are given below, but each situation calls for individual study and prayer. There may be few visible results, but such results do occur and, seen or unseen, can be measured in

terms of angels rejoicing in heaven "over one sinner who

repents" (Luke 15:10). Our evangelism efforts proceed from the love of God in Jesus Christ, undeterred by fear of failure, for the Word of God is never spoken in vain. God promises that His Word will not return empty but will accomplish what He desires and achieve the purposes for which He sent it (Isaiah 55:10–11).

THE JOY OF EVANGELISM IN ACTION

The challenge of evangelizing New Agers should move Christians to intense study of the Word of God. To know the certainty of one's own salvation through faith in Christ as revealed in the Word of God is the first requirement for giving an effective witness. The Christian evangelist will want to grow beyond knowing the simple facts of salvation in order to make full use of the power of "the whole counsel of God" (Acts 20:27). Moreover, as Christians study the Word of God, they grow not only in knowledge but in grace and power, resulting in blessings that they will discover again and again in their own daily living.

Prayer forms such a vital part of the Christian's life that it hardly seems necessary to emphasize it in connection with evangelism. But do Christians ever spend enough time in prayer? The prelude to evangelizing is prayer. The work of evangelism is done with more prayer. And the follow-up is still more prayer.

71

An *expectant heart* is essential for the Christian evangelist. He or she must operate with the truth that no one is beyond the reach of the Holy Spirit. Every individual is part of the world that "God so loved . . . that He gave His only Son" to redeem (John 3:16). Many thousands of the redeemed, now and all eternity, praise God because He sent them an evangelist who in the power of the Holy Spirit undertook an "impossible" task. If it should please God to let you see a soul delivered from darkness into the light of Christ, it is a special blessing indeed. On the other hand, you may be totally unaware of how the Holy Spirit is working through your testimony.

An evangelist must at all times *display patience and Christian love.* A Christian has no right to be unkind to someone who holds beliefs other than his or her own. The followers of the New Age Movement (especially the occult form) often consider committed Christians to be their greatest adversaries. An impatient or arrogant

Steps for Evangelizing New Agers

1. Study the Word of God.
2. Pray.
3. Have an expectant heart.
4. Display Christian patience and love.
5. Don't be afraid to listen and learn.
6. Tell what Jesus has done for you.

attitude will widen the cultural, social, or religious concerns that may have led such people to the New Age Movement in the first place. Overt verbal attacks or ridicule will only strengthen their conviction that something is wrong with established Christianity.

Don't be afraid to listen and learn. By listening, the evangelist may grasp the hungers that led a particular person into the New Age Movement. Through such awareness, the evangelist can then know what Word of God to bring to bear on a particular human condition.

Tell what Jesus has done for you. In one case you may talk to a stranger who has already been "immunized" against the Christian religion. In another case you may be fearful of intruding upon the life of a co-worker or friend. In either event, it is helpful to know as much as possible about the person's involvement in the New Age Movement, but it is not necessary. Attention should not be focused on variations of the New Age theme. Nor are you called to defend your church or denomination or the Christian religion. What is essential is your confession that Jesus Christ found and saved you and has given you great joy and security. Be prepared to give simple, clear confession of your faith—in a cordial and nonaccusing manner.

Remember that the New Age Movement in both its occult and humanist expressions does not acknowledge sin. Sin is not considered a moral problem but merely ignorance of inherent human divinity and is to be overcome through experiential "enlightenment." Tell of your nature as a sinful human being and how God has redeemed you from that sin. Explain that this redemption does not depend on meditation, lifestyle, psychological techniques, or the word of the latest teacher. Remember, too, that nothing the New Age offers can compare with God's great Easter event.

In his or her innermost heart, the New Ager with whom you speak may be yearning for the same peace, joy, and security that you display. Under God's grace he or she may be reached by your sincere and patient speaking of the Good News. In giving instructions to Christian evangelists, the apostle Peter said, "Always [be] prepared to make a defense to anyone who asks you for a reason for the hope that is in you . . ." Then he added, "Yet do it with gentleness and respect" (1 Peter 3:15).

The New Age Movement demonstrates, perhaps more than any other contemporary religious phenomenon, that the basic human disease has not changed. People still want to "be like God" (Genesis 3:5)—not in personal holiness but in unlimited power. Therefore, the remedy also has not changed: the magnificent transformation brought about by the Gospel.

A word of challenge rings through an article by Craig V. Anderson:

> Shirley MacLaine is an easy target. . . . More to the point, how do our efforts shape up in the eyes of the one who knows our every move and motive? What about our spiritual hungers? Do we seek to deepen our awareness of the eternal? And having sought to know God, do we then share our discoveries with our brothers and sisters, so that they too can be edified? Having been in the presence of the holy, are we passionately engaged with our companions on this planet?[3]

A concluding word from God is especially appropriate:

> And we know that the Son of God has come and has given us understanding, so that we may know Him who is true; and we are in Him who is true, in His Son Jesus Christ. He is the true God and eternal life.

> Little children, keep yourselves from idols. (1 John 5:20–21)

RESOURCES

CHRISTIAN RESOURCES ON THE NEW AGE

Chandler, Russell. *Understanding the New Age.* Grand Rapids: Zondervan, 1993.

Groothuis, Douglas R. *Unmasking the New Age.* Downers Grove, IL: InterVarsity Press, 1986.

Martin, Walter. *The New Age Cult.* Minneapolis: Bethany House, 1989.

Smith, Warren. *The Light That Was Dark: From the New Age to Amazing Grace.* Magnalia, CA: Mountain Stream Press, 2005.

New Age Resources

Editors of *Body, Mind & Spirit* magazine. *The New Age Catalog.* New York: Doubleday, 1988.

Ferguson, Marilyn. *The Aquarian Conspiracy.* New York: Penguin, 2009.

Humanist Manifestos I and II. Buffalo: Prometheus Books, 1973.

Internet Resources

www.lcms.org (See the Commission on Theology and Church Relation page for an excellent summary of New Age thought.)

www.lucistrust.org/en (Lucis Trust has been a prominent New Age organization from almost the beginning of the movement.)

Pew Forum on Religious and Public Life, "Many Americans Mix Multiple Faiths" (December 2009). pewforum.org/docs/?DocIC=490

NOTES
CHAPTER ONE

1. See Constance Cumbey, *The Hidden Dangers of the Rainbow*, rev. ed. (Shreveport, LA: Huntington House, 1985); M. Scott Peck, *The Road Less Traveled;* Texe Marrs, *Mystery Mark of the New Age* (Westchester, IL: Crossway, 1988); and Marilyn Ferguson, *The Aquarian Conspiracy* (New York: Penguin, 2009).
2. Quoted in Walter Martin, *The New Age Cult* (Minneapolis: Bethany House, 1989), 25–26.
3. Ferguson, *Aquarian Conspiracy*, 158–63.
4. Ferguson, *Aquarian Conspiracy*, 85–87.

CHAPTER TWO

1. Don Matzat, *Inner Healing* (Eugene, OR: Harvest House, 1987), 158.
2. Mary Baker Eddy, *Science and Health with Key to the Scriptures* (Boston: Allison V. Stewart, 1918), 468.
3. John C. Cooper, *Religious Pied Pipers* (Valley Forge, PA: Judson Press, 1981), 91.

CHAPTER THREE

1. Pew Forum on Religious and Public Life, "Many Americans Mix Multiple Faiths" (December 2009), 2.
2. Russell Chandler, *Understanding the New Age* (Dallas: Word Publishing, 1988), 244.
3. Elliot Miller, "Parliament of the World's Religions," *Christian Research Journal* 16:2 (Fall 1993): 11.
4. Eldon Winker, *The New Age Is Lying to You* (St. Louis: Concordia, 1994), 70–71.

CHAPTER FOUR

1. David Spangler, "Defining the New Age," *The New Age Catalogue* (New York: Doubleday, 1988), n.p., emphasis added.

2. Confirmed by Caryl Matrisciana in 1983 and quoted in her *Gods of the New Age* (Eugene, OR: Harvest House, 1985), 170–71.

3. Quoted in Douglas R. Groothuis, *Unmasking the New Age* (Downers Grove, IL: Intervarsity Press, 1986), 14; emphasis added.

4. Father Maury Smith, *A Practical Guide to Value Clarification* (La Jolla, CA: University Associates, 1977), 5.

5. Smith, *Practical Guide*, 210.

6. Ferguson, *Aquarian Controversy*, 128.

7. Robert Muller, *New Genesis* (Garden City, NY: Doubleday, 1982), 152.

CHAPTER FIVE

1. Marilyn Ferguson, *The Aquarian Conspiracy* (New York: Penguin, 2009), 35, 217.

CHAPTER SIX

1. Douglas R. Groothuis, *Unmasking the New Age* (Downers Grove, IL: Intervarsity Press, 1986), 174.

2. Marilyn Ferguson, *The Aquarian Conspiracy* (New York: Penguin, 2009), 28.

3. Craig V. Anderson, n.t., *The Christian Century* (February 25, 1987).

Notes

Notes